# Silly Aunt Tilly

written by Jennifer Jacobson
illustrated by Tuko Fujisaki

**HARCOURT BRACE & COMPANY**
Orlando Atlanta Austin Boston San Francisco Chicago Dallas New York
Toronto London

My Aunt Tilly went to
the North Pole one day.
She left me behind,
I am sad to say.

She shared a ride with a polar bear.

He showed her how to fish from a chair.

Aunt Tilly came home
with birds in her hair.
And she brought
something back for me.

A snowball packed in
ice cubes.
Silly Aunt Tilly!

My Aunt Tilly went to
the rain forest one day.
She left me behind,
I am sad to say.

She shared a ride
with a chimpanzee.

He showed her how to swing from a tree.

Aunt Tilly came home
with bees in her hair.
And she brought
something back for me.

A blue-spotted bird's egg.
Silly Aunt Tilly!

My Aunt Tilly went to
the city one day.
She left me behind,
I am sad to say.

She shared a ride with
a big, green fish.

He showed her how to
eat without a dish.

Aunt Tilly came home with
a crown in her hair.
And she brought
something back for me.

Thank you Aunt Tilly!

# For Michael, Love Cynda

by Cynda Yeasting

FriesenPress

Suite 300 - 990 Fort St
Victoria, BC, Canada, V8V 3K2
www.friesenpress.com


First Edition — 2016



Disclaimer: This book is based on true events to the best of my recollection. These are my memories and I am the narrator of my own story. The real names of family members have been used as their names are already listed in the online obituary and also cross-referenced in other searches on the internet. To protect the privacy of others, names and places may have been removed or changed. Any resemblance to a living person with the same or similar name is purely coincidental.

**ISBN**
978-1-4602-6747-9 (Hardcover)
978-1-4602-6748-6 (Paperback)
978-1-4602-6749-3 (eBook)

*1. Biography & Autobiography, Personal Memoirs*

Distributed to the trade by The Ingram Book Company